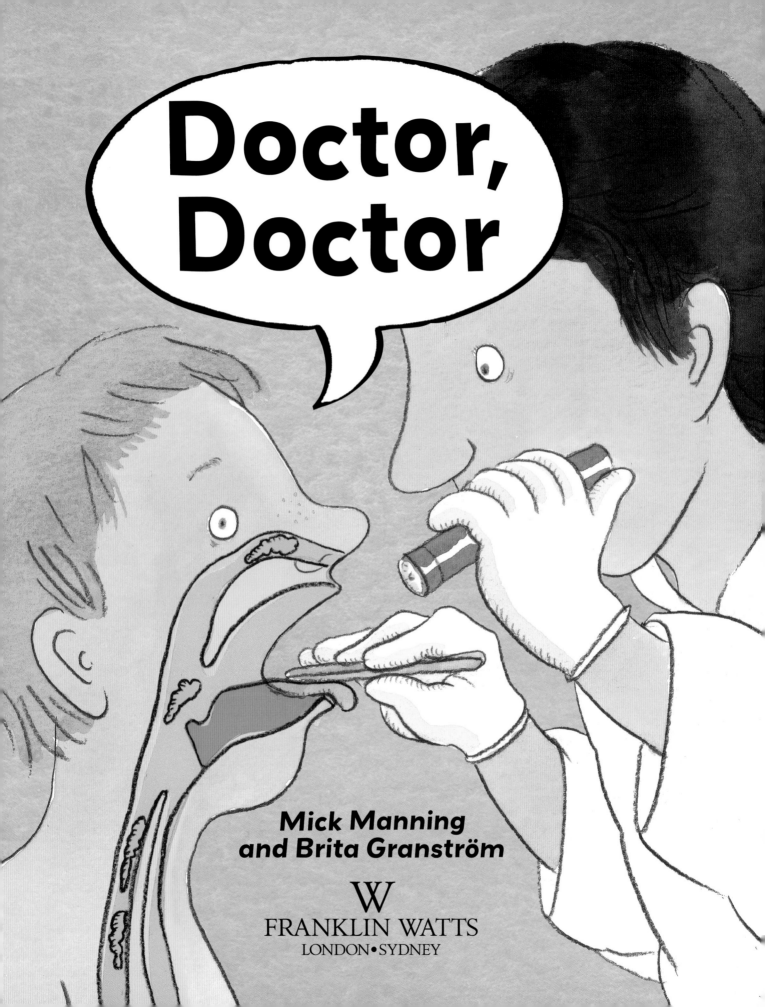

'Agh, my leg!'

Chen was tackled hard at football. His leg is really sore and he can hardly walk. What could it be?

A twisted ankle?

Your ankle joint can move in many directions, but you can accidentally bend or twist it too far. Then it swells up with fluid and is painful to move.

A broken leg?

A bad fall or sharp blow can break a leg bone - and that hurts even more! There will be a lot of swelling and bruising and it will be very painful to put weight on the leg.

An x-ray takes a photograph of inside people's bodies. It will show if a bone is broken.

Shall we x-ray his leg?

Let's ask the new Doc. What do you think?

5

The Doc says

Tom's cold has led to a chest infection. To clear it up, Tom must take a course of antibiotics for a week. Bacteria and viruses are called germs. They mix with the mucus you sneeze out and cough up. This spreads germs so use a tissue to catch the gunk - and remember to wash your hands.

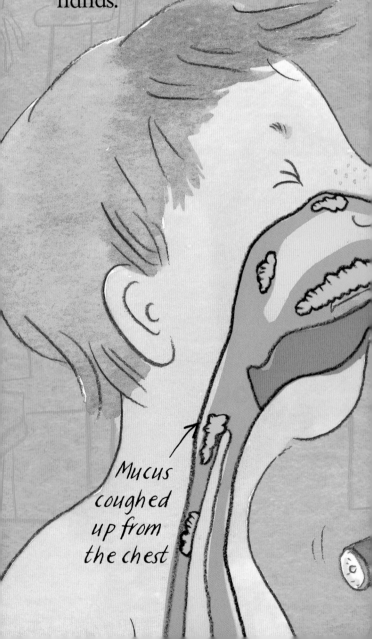

Mucus coughed up from the chest

'I've got a cold'

Tom has got a sore throat and a snotty nose. He can't stop sneezing and his chest feels sore. What could it be?

Just a cold?

A cold is a viral infection. It can affect your nose, ears or throat. Your body makes mucus or 'gunk' to get rid of the virus but this makes you cough and sneeze. There's no medicine to cure a cold.

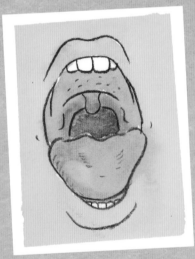

Your throat often looks red and sore when you get a cold.

A chest infection?

Sometimes, with a bad cold, the gunk in your chest gets infected with bacteria. You may have a high temperature and chest pains. Drugs called antibiotics destroy bacteria.

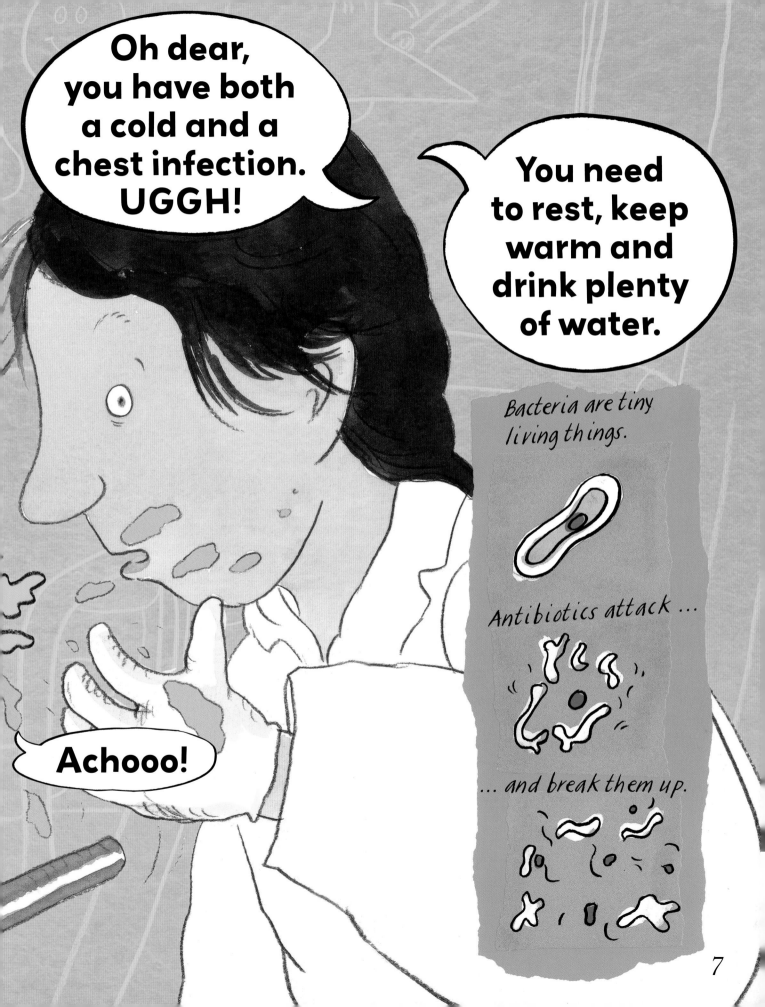

'I'm all spotty!'

Freya feels itchy and she's got red spots popping up all over! She has a temperature, too and has lost her appetite. What could it be?

Chicken pox?

Chicken pox is a common itchy, spotty virus we can all catch from each other; at school, at home, almost anywhere in fact!

Measles?

Measles isn't so common now as most children are innoculated with an MMR jab (measles, mumps and rubella). When measles does crop up, it is painful and can make people very ill.

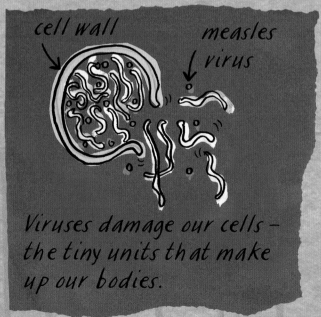

cell wall   measles
virus

Viruses damage our cells – the tiny units that make up our bodies.

Hmm! Take a look at those spots!

9

'I cut my head'

Freddie fell off his bike. It's obvious to the doctor and nurse that he has cut his head - but how will they treat his wound?

Doctor's glue?

This is a strong, medical glue that sticks the edges of the wound together until it heals. It comes in a special glue pen that only doctors can use.

A stitch?

A gaping wound needs to be stitched together to help it heal. The special thread used slowly dissolves as the wound heals.

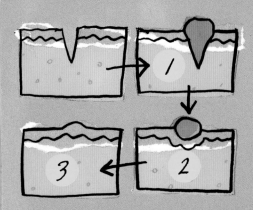

Healing begins with a clot (1); a scab forms (2) as the blood dries. Underneath the skin regrows (3).

'I'm so tired'

Mo is thirsty and needs to go to the toilet all the time! He's very tired too, and has lost a lot of weight . . .

Is it anaemia?

Anaemia is a lack of iron and other nutrients in the blood - it makes you feel tired and weak. It helps to eat foods rich in iron. They include oily fish, red meat, green veg, beans and even chocolate!

Is it diabetes?

This disease causes high blood sugar that leads to thirst, weight loss and tiredness. It can be very dangerous but thankfully modern treatments help people live with it.

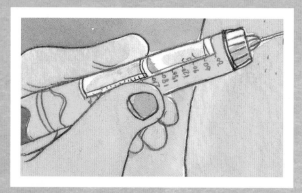

Diabetics use a special pen to give themselves injections of insulin everyday.

I'm taking blood samples to send off to a lab.

The Doc says

Diabetes is an illness where the body does not make enough insulin. Insulin in our blood turns the natural sugar in our food into the energy we need. Without insulin the sugar builds up in the blood and this is very dangerous.

Mo must learn to inject insulin and regularly test his blood sugar levels himself. There is no cure for diabetes but, with care, diabetics can live normally.

A very high reading indeed. I think you're diabetic.

Our diabetic specialist will help Mo.

'I can't breathe'

Jed's finding it hard to breathe, particularly during PE or if he's in a rush. And sometimes he wheezes at night and his chest hurts. What could it be?

A chest infection?

This can make you wheezy and your lungs hurt. Has the patient got a runny nose or a temperature?

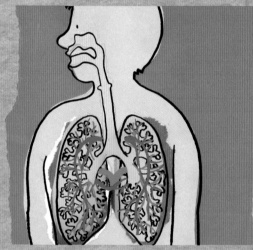

We breathe air into our lungs. Air spreads through these two expandable bags in a network of tiny airways.

Asthma?

Asthma swells the airways that take air around your lungs, making it hard to breathe. You can feel tight across your chest and short of breath, especially when doing sports.

14

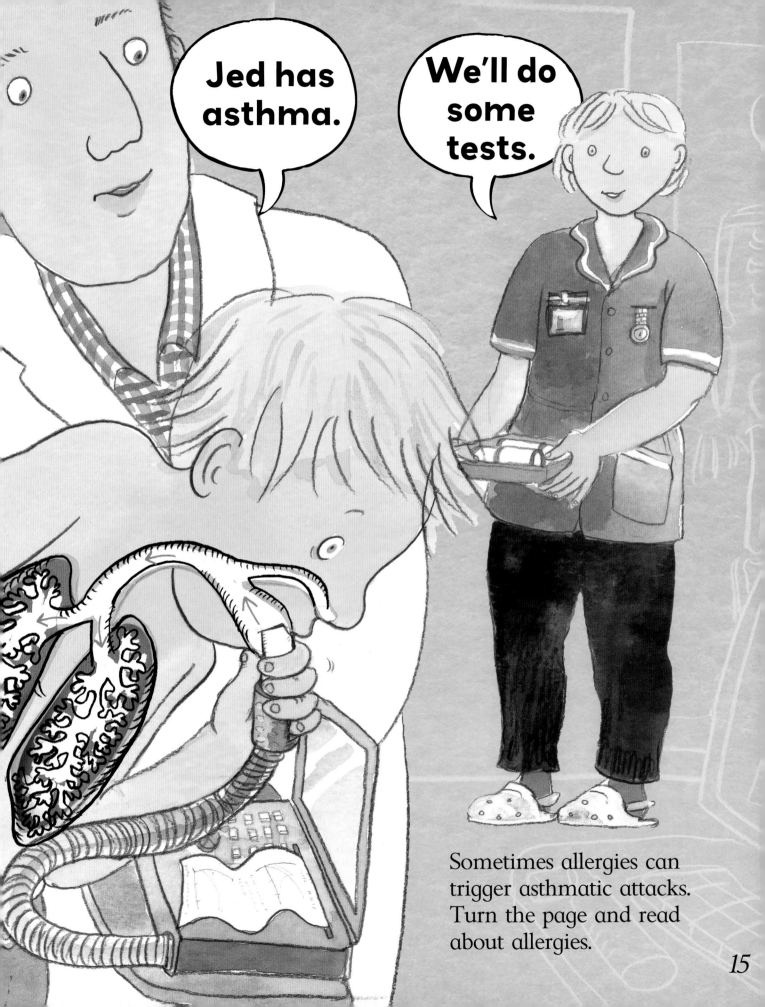

Sometimes allergies can trigger asthmatic attacks. Turn the page and read about allergies.

15

'I'm all dizzy'

Lucy has been for a picnic in the country. She picked flowers and ate peanut butter sandwiches. Now her hand is swollen. She's also got a red rash and she is sneezing and feels dizzy. What could it be?

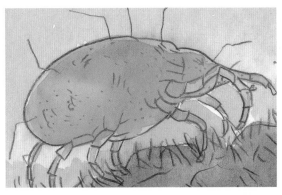

Dust mites cause allergies. They like our modern, warm houses.

1 Cats
2 Dust mites
3 Mould
4 Wasp stings
5 Pollen from flowers
6 Peanuts
7 Shellfish
8 Milk
9 Wheat
10 Soya

The Doc says

Allergies are becoming more common - perhaps because we've become cleaner! Allergies to pollen and dust mites make people sneeze and their eyes get runny and itchy. Foods like nuts and shellfish can cause serious allergic reactions, so Lucy must be very careful as her tests show she has, amongst other things, a peanut allergy.

17

'I have chest pains'

Jim's granny is overweight and doesn't take any exercise. She's been getting neck pain, chest pains and shortness of breath for a while, but it suddenly got worse this morning. What's happening?

Indigestion?

Eating your food too quickly can give you 'heartburn', a pain around the chest. It doesn't usually last very long.

Heart attack?

Granny's symptoms, along with high blood pressure, may be a sign of heart disease. She could be having a heart attack.

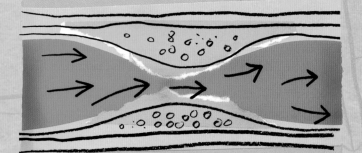

Fat can build up in blood vessels as cholesterol. This stops the heart beating properly and causes high blood pressure.

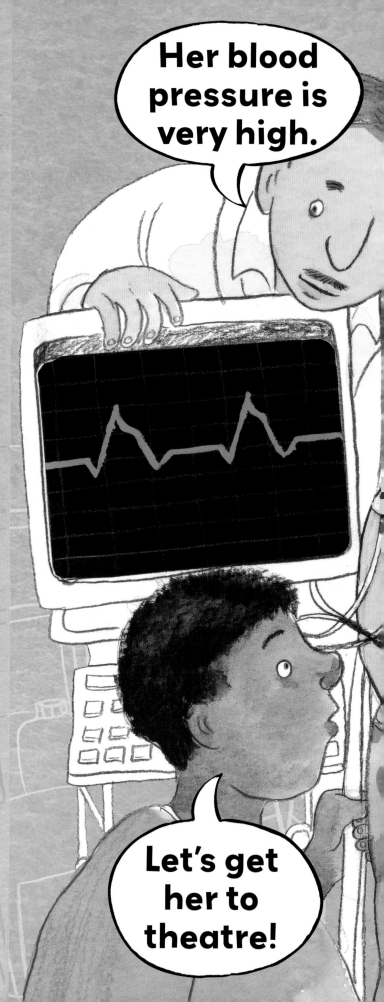

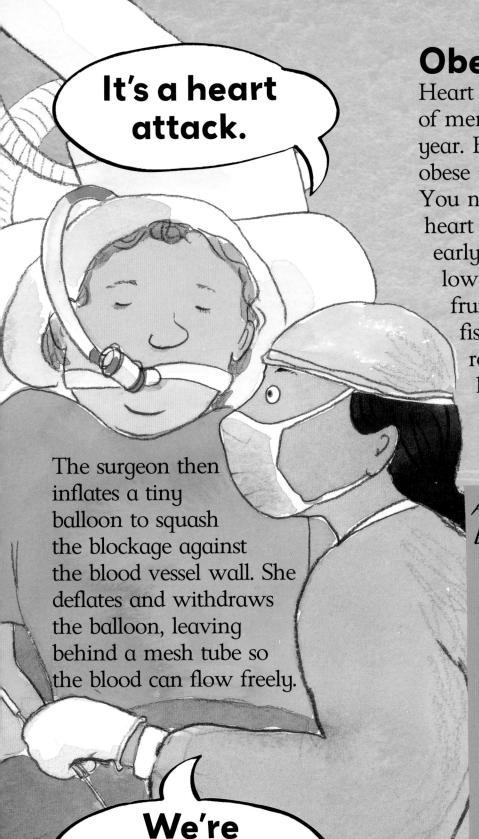

It's a heart attack.

The surgeon then inflates a tiny balloon to squash the blockage against the blood vessel wall. She deflates and withdraws the balloon, leaving behind a mesh tube so the blood can flow freely.

We're performing an angioplasty.

Obesity

Heart disease kills thousands of men and women every year. Being overweight - or obese - is a major cause. You need to look after your heart and your body from an early age. Aim for a low fat, low sugar diet; rich in fresh fruit and vegetables, oily fish, like sardines, and roughage from cereals, like oats and bran. Don't eat too much though and, of course, take regular exercise, too.

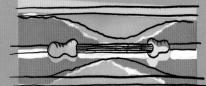

An angioplasty clears a blocked blood vessel.

1. A tiny tube is pushed through the blockage.

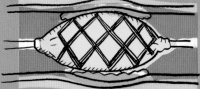

2. Balloon inflated.

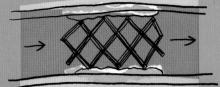

3. Mesh left behind.

19

The Doc says

Small children can easily swallow tiny things they put in their mouth. If it blocks the 'wind pipe' it can stop their breathing, if it goes down the 'food pipe' it ends up in the tummy. Sometime doctors have to operate - but luckily for Zack, this key will come out in a day or two naturally . . . in his poo!

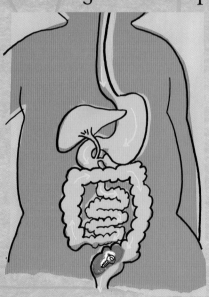

Our digestive system breaks up our food so our body can use its goodness and energy. Any waste it can't digest, like a key, comes out as poo.

'My tummy hurts'

Little Zack is feeling poorly. He started coughing and choking but he wasn't sick. Now he says his tummy is sore. What could it be?

A tummy bug?

Children can pick up the common germs that cause a tummy bug anywhere. A sore tummy, sickness and runny poo are obvious signs of a tummy bug.

Sometimes being sick helps get rid of the germs.

Swallowed something?

Small children are always putting things into their mouths as a way of 'feeling them'. Could Zack have swallowed something?

20

Sorry we're late, Doctor. I couldn't find my house key!

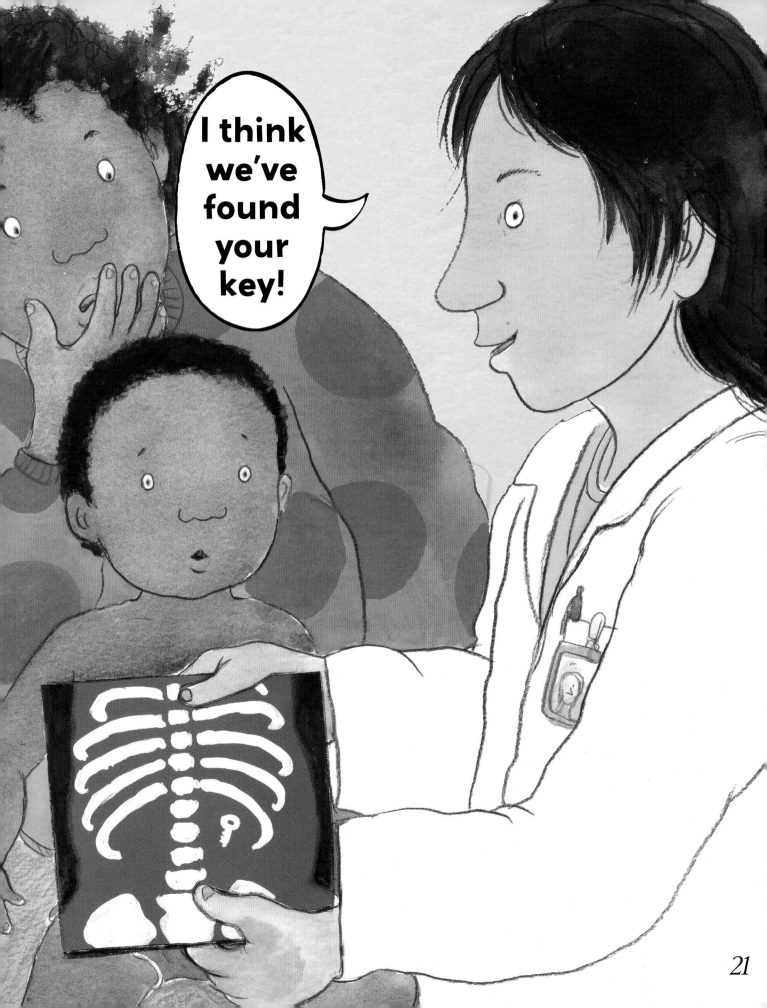

21

Full recovery!

We all need to look after ourselves. We can all do this by exercising more - through walking or sports. We should also make sure we eat a healthy diet of fresh fruit and veg, cereals, fish and lean meat, cutting down on cakes, sweets, sugary drinks and fast food.

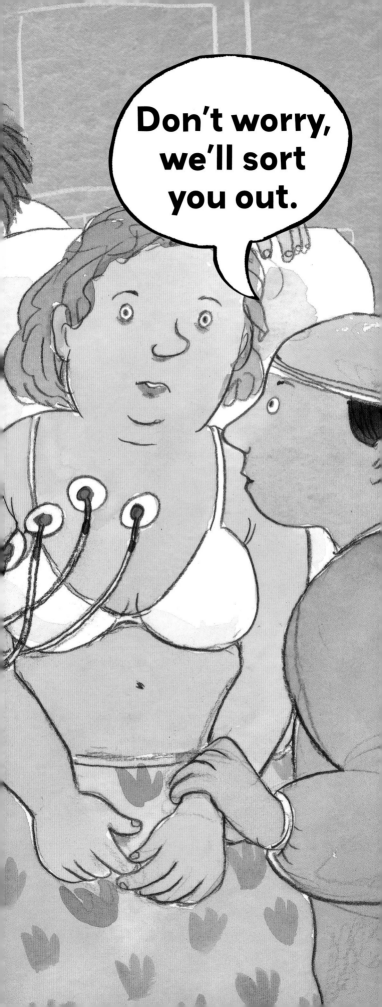

The Doc says

One of Granny's blood vessels has become completely blocked, causing a 'heart attack'. Watching on the TV screen, a heart surgeon pushes a tube along a blood vessel in her arm until it reaches the blockage.

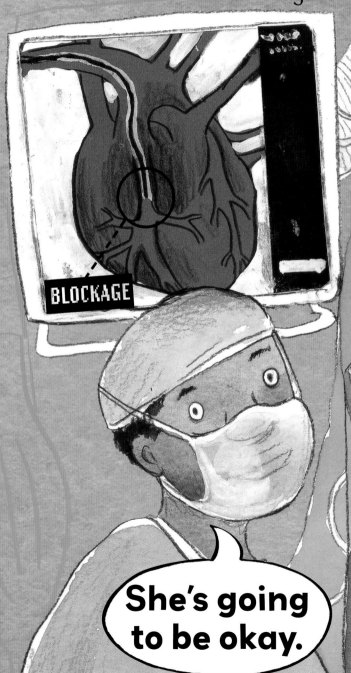

BLOCKAGE

She's going to be okay.

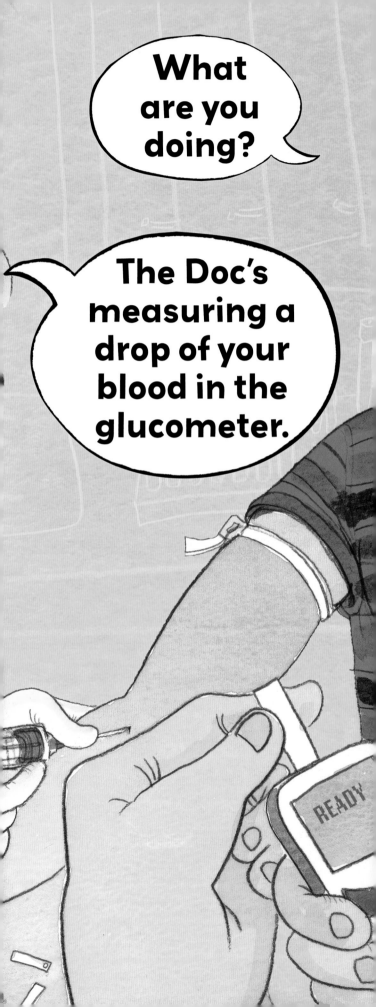

The Doc says

Asthma is a disease of the lungs. You can't catch it, it's just something you have. Symptoms are usually worse at night and first thing in the morning. Asthma attacks happen when the airways suddenly get very tight.

This spirometer measures how much air Jed can breathe into his lungs.

People with asthma breathe in medicine from inhalers.

The Doc says

Our body is covered in skin. It acts as a protective barrier and is full of nerves and blood vessels. When you cut yourself, new skin grows within a few days.

A bad cut needs help healing; sometimes a plaster stitch is enough, but this one needs some 'doctor's glue'.

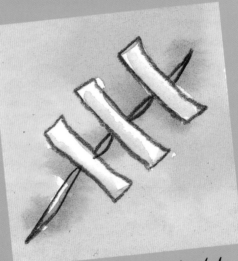

A plaster stitch holds a small cut together so it heals.

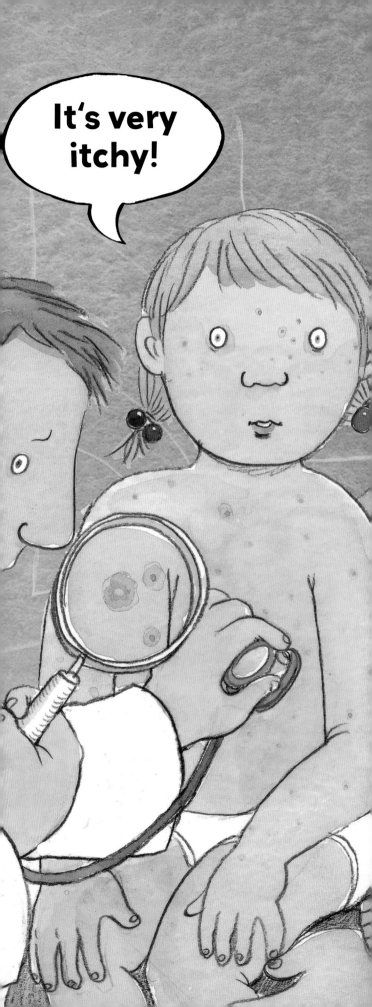

The Doc says

Chicken pox is a common virus. The itchy spots become blisters that burst, crust over and then heal in about 5 days. Chicken pox is a virus, so antibiotics (see page 6) won't help.

Don't scratch itchy spots. A lotion like Calamine helps soothe them.

Your body gets rid of a virus on its own. White blood cells fight back and destroy 'invaders' like viruses.

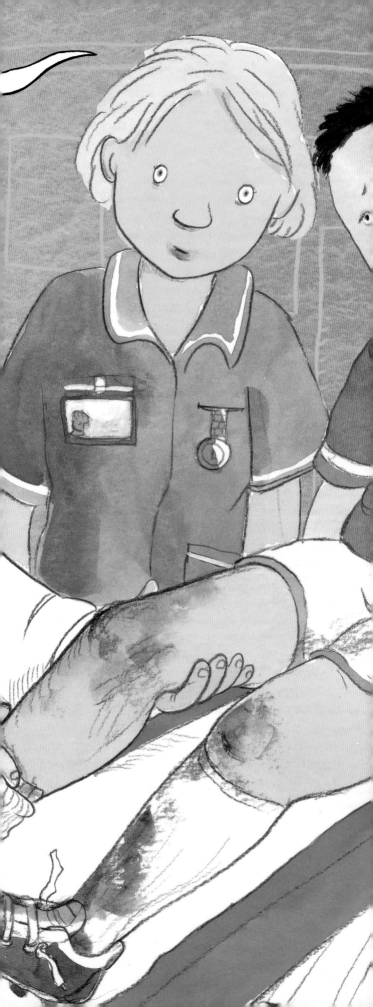

The Doc says

Chen has a hairline fracture - a thin, neat break. A multiple fracture, with lots of broken bits, would be much worse. Chen must have the bone set - straightened and put 'in plaster'. He will wear the plaster for a few weeks until the bone grows back together.

A plaster of Paris bandage or 'pot' sets rock hard.

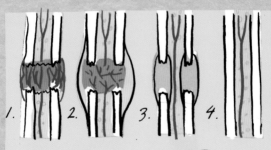

1.   2.   3.   4.

Bone mends itself.
1. Broken bone.
2-3. Growing back together.
4. Good as new!

Index

For the hard working doctors and nurses at Berwick Hospital, Well Close Surgery and Borders General.

First published in 2008 by Franklin Watts,
338 Euston Road, London, NW1 3BH

Franklin Watts Australia
Level 17/207 Kent Road, Sydney, NSW 2000

Text and illustrations © 2008
Mick Manning and Brita Granström

Brita made the illustrations
for this book
Find out more about Mick and Brita on
www.mickandbrita.com

Editor: Rachel Cooke
Art director: Jonathan Hair

Consultants: Dr Barry Warner,
Peter Riley

Printed in China
A CIP catalogue record is available
from the British Library.

Dewey Classification: 616

ISBN: 978 0 7496 7818 0

Franklin Watts is a division of
Hachette Children's Books,
an Hachette Livre UK company.
www.hachettelivre.co.uk